Quarantine

What People Can Learn from the Craziest Year Ever

BY

ALEXA BOWERS

QUARANTINE

Copyright © 2021 by Alexa Bowers.

All rights reserved. No part of this publication may be reproduced, distributed, or transmitted in any form or by any means, including photocopying, recording, or other electronic or mechanical methods, without the prior written permission of the author, except in the case of brief quotations embodied in critical reviews and certain other non-commercial uses permitted by copyright law.

Ordering Information: Quantity sales. Special discounts are available on quantity purchases by corporations, associations, and others. Orders by U.S. trade bookstores and wholesalers.

www.DreamStartersPublishing.com

ALEXA BOWERS

Table of Contents

Introduction 4

What People Would Do During Quarantine 7

How People Would Feel and How They Spent Their Time . 13

Positive Mindset 18

Conscious vs. Subconscious Mind 23

How We Are More Powerful Together 27

When You Lose Things You Take for Granted 32

How Reading & Writing Helps You Feed Your Brain 37

How Balance Was Important 42

Using the Pandemic as an Excuse 47

Quarantine Coming to an End 52

ABOUT THE AUTHOR 58

Introduction

Why I Wrote This Book

I wrote this book because everything was shut down including schools, stores, work and basically everything. I really had nothing to do, so I started to write and write. Next thing I knew I wrote chapters and coming closer and closer to getting a book done. It was not easy, but once I finished the book it felt amazing, and it was really fun to accomplish. Writing this book actually made me think more about how this global pandemic helped me to focus on a goal and stop and think what everyone was going through. I wrote this book at first for something to do to keep me going, but then I realized how this might help other kids and families.

Who Should Read This?

Really anyone can read this book. It is for all ages. You can not only learn about what my family went through, but about motivation and mindset. You can read this as an adult or even if you are little and just learning to read, you can read the book with your parents. This book is not just meant for kids or adults. Remember, it is for all ages. Read it with your kids & have discussions as a family. Read it alone and make your own thoughts and ideas.

What Will You Learn?

You can learn about motivation and how to set a goal and strive to accomplish it. Also, you can learn about my perspective of the outcome of Covid-19 as a kid and how I saw this hard and stressful time through my eyes. Not only do I talk about my family, but I try to talk about the present time as it was during the days ahead and what really happened. You can take as much as you want out of it, but it is meant to see this crazy pandemic from the eyes of a 12-year-old and to not waste precious time.

How To Get the Most Out of This Book

You can get the most out of my book by taking notes and rereading if you can't quite understand something. Also, throughout the book there are sections to write down your takeaways from each the chapter. This can help you understand the content, why you are reading it and what you can apply to your daily life. Take your time, have fun learning and read alone or with a friend or family member!

QUARANTINE

What is Covid-19?

The coronavirus was first detected in Wuhan, China, in late 2019 and has set off a global pandemic. Experts say SARS-CoV-2 (Covid19) originated in bats. As it began to rapidly spread to the Human Population, our entire World, the communities we live and work in, began to shut down and we were told to stay at home to prevent the spread of this virus. You can find out more information on Covid19/SARS-CoV-2 by visiting websites like www.kidsheath.org / www.healthychildren.org / www.hopkinsmedicine.org / www.mayoclinic.org

Chapter 1

What People Would Do During Quarantine

One time in the world there was a disease that was brought to everyone's attention. This disease was COVID-19. I know what people did during Quarantine, they STAYED HOME. I am only 12 years old, but I still know how crazy this all was, because we had to get out of school and parents/adults had to work from home and we all had to stay at home.

During Quarantine it was different, if you saw friends and family you would have to be six feet apart and wear a mask and gloves. Kids who were younger than me and older

QUARANTINE

than me were still doing schoolwork and staying inside their houses. That doesn't mean that you stopped living your life, though.

We may have to be at home, but that doesn't mean that you must change your life because of this new way of daily life. You should never stop living your life. Until you let anything else or anyone else put you down, just remember it's all in your head. Just because a negative thought in your mind is telling you to do something YOU get to choose your destiny.

All of us at first were scared and were constantly buying things like gloves, masks, hand sanitizer, and even sanitized delivery boxes. Everyone was buying these things like the world was ending and we could never leave our homes again. I remember this one time when I went to the store with my mom. We needed to buy gloves, masks etc., but when you went to the shelves, they were bare. It was scary at times not being able to have access to the supplies we needed because we didn't know how long the shutdown would last.

No one really knew what was happening because no one experienced a pandemic before. For example, we did not know how many supplies we needed to buy before stores closed and even what would be left in stores the next day when shopping. Times were tough and it was hard to get what you needed, but it was important to make sure to provide for your family, loved ones and yourself.

ALEXA BOWERS

Looking back, it has made me realize how lucky we are to have access to things we need now. I can still remember that I was not in a store for about 80 days. I would either stay home or wait in the car, because it would feel like a safe haven whenever my parents had to go into stores.

Next, there were not a lot of things to do. Camps and daycares were shut down and parents still had to work. It was a very hard time for some people because they did not always know what to do with their kids. There were lots of people who were constantly watching the news to keep up to date about the illness. There were lots of people who sadly passed during this time but, you still must look on the bright side of Covid – 19. If this virus would not have ever happened, I would not be as close with my aunt, uncle and cousin. It is important to think of something that you can look on the bright side.

Another thing about quarantine is that it was not all bad. I don't know about everyone else, but I know my family got closer because we all wanted to be together more. We thought, why don't the six of us all stay quarantined together? I was elated that we were quarantined together because I felt like I had a sister and if my parents were working, I basically had two other parents I could be with. Most of the time people only look at terrible things that came out of COVID, but you also must look at positives.

This was all something that we had never seen or heard of before. Therefore, there was so much caution with

QUARANTINE

everything we did. Not even doctors or nurses knew what this was. This whole virus showed me that everything has a silver lining. The whole thing may have been a good thing for some people to realize there is always a positive side to a negative situation and you may just have to try harder to figure it out. Also, don't forget to set goals and try hard. People could have used this time to make changes, stand up and set goals, or people could have just done nothing and stopped living their life just because of a setback. You should never let a setback stop you.

What did you take away from this chapter?

1.

2.

3.

QUARANTINE

TIP #1

Always stay active and working, even if you don't feel like you have to, because you never know if that could be taken away.

Chapter 2

How People Would Feel and How They Spent Their Time

There were some people who felt amazing at home and some people who felt like they had to get out. When this all started, people would mostly work and do schoolwork at home, known as "virtual learning". Once school was done kids would either see their friends 6 feet apart outside or they would FaceTime each other. Even sports were cancelled for a long time. I don't know about everyone else, but I love sports because they keep us healthy, active and they are just fun. Quarantine was hard sometimes and not fun because we

QUARANTINE

were stuck in our house, but at least I had my loving and caring family with me.

I am not going to look back on these times and say, "Wow, everything about Covid was terrible." I am going to look back and say, "There were some ups and downs, but we eventually got through it together." I know these times were very hard for some people with the loss of jobs, income concerns and health and safety of loved ones, but we always have to try to find the bright side.

People definitely do not enjoy being forced to be stuck inside at home. This year was very different, and we did miss out on a lot of things, but the most important lesson I learned was to focus on keeping myself, my friends and family safe and happy.

One thing that was different was the holidays. A lot of families either had Zoom parties with each other or just spent the holidays inside. Some people were sadly home sick or just home with nothing to do. It was hard to go places, so for Christmas we had to Zoom video call to some of our family.

Luckily, some of my grandparents lived nearby so I actually got to see them, after quarantining, of course. It was a good Christmas, but not the same as normal. Usually we go Black Friday shopping, but we couldn't. To make the holidays a little better for everyone, I made sure to put a lot of thought into everyone's gifts, so they all knew how important they were to me.

ALEXA BOWERS

Not everyone thought of 2020 as the best time, but some did. I always say that YOU HAVE TO LOOK ON THE BRIGHT SIDE. You can't always focus on the negative, you need to think of some positive things. I am not saying for everyone to ignore your feelings, but instead to turn those bad memories into good memories.

For example, we were stuck at home, so my cousin, aunt and uncle moved in for a little bit. Personally, 2020 was a really good year for me because my cousin/best friend moved 3 houses down from me and I got a dog. I tried to make agendas for the days, even throughout school, to spend some time with my cousin and make this year memorable for her.

She was just starting kindergarten and had just moved to a new area. I did my best to keep her active and have fun, so I would come up with fun things to do with her, or give her things to do on her own, while I had schoolwork to do. She always felt like a little sister to me, so I knew it was my responsibility to make her feel comfortable and happy here.

It was also important to remember that there are plenty of ways to have fun and live life while being safe. You could still go outside and ride bikes or hike, you can still FaceTime and call your friends, or just drive to a vacation instead of fly. You always have to try to turn negative things into positives!

QUARANTINE

What did you take away from this chapter?

1.

2.

3.

TIP #2:

Don't just focus on the negatives, try to find the positive in every situation.

Chapter 3

Positive Mindset

It is very important to have a growth mindset about all of this. If we turn some of those sad memories into new happy memories people will be happier. I would like to give you some exercises to keep a positive mindset and ideas no matter what your age is.

- **Wake up early** – A good time to get your day started is from 5-6am. You can do that with an alarm clock or wake up by yourself. Also, what will help you get up is to put your alarm clock across your room so that you have to get out of bed to turn it off.
- **Exercise -** Some exercises that are good for you are running, biking, meditating, workout classes and

way more. For kids, you can look up videos of workouts and try them at home. When you exercise, the goal is to get your blood going and your brain going. If you wake up early and do these exercises you will feel good for the rest of the day because you woke up early and worked out.

- **Your Mind -** Your mind is important because if you get your mind right and your body right then you will set yourself up to be successful. A quote I really love is, "If you are willing to do only what's easy, life will be hard. But, if you are willing to do what's hard, life will be easy." This quote is by T. Harv Eker. This quote is saying to do the hard things first and it will get easier, rather than doing easy things first. There are two parts of your mind, and they are conscious and subconscious. In the next chapter I will be talking more about the conscious and subconscious mind.

A positive mindset got me through quarantine because I did not always want to get on the computer and "go to school," but I did end up doing it because I thought about all of the positive things, like how I need to learn and see my friends and teachers. I also did not always enjoy having to stay in my home the whole time, but I needed to be safe.

QUARANTINE

Another way I had a positive mindset was by working out every morning to get my brain going. Some days I just didn't want to work out, but my dad motivated me to do it and reminded me that I do this all the time to stay healthy and happy. Michael Jordan is a big inspiration for me, and his quotes have always kept me on track with my goals.

What did you take away from this chapter?

1.
_____
_____
_____
_____

2.
_____
_____
_____
_____

3.
_____
_____
_____
_____

TIP #3:

Growth mindsets lead to success and positive habits, so always push yourself to new limits.

Chapter 4

Conscious vs. Subconscious Mind

The conscious mind is where all of your thoughts, feelings and memories are. The subconscious mind is like being on autopilot. For example, think about when you brush your teeth - your body knows what to do, you don't really have to tell it how to brush your teeth every time. Both parts of the mind are extremely important but are used in different ways for different things.

It is important to have a strong conscious mind because it means that you are aware of yourself and others around you. Our subconscious mind is constantly focused on the present moment. Since we don't use our conscious mind as much, it makes it easy to create excuses for ourselves.

QUARANTINE

For example, our subconscious mind will say "I will be successful" rather than using our conscious mind to say "I am successful."

Before the discovery of electricity, the only source of light was by fire. If it wasn't for Thomas Edison and his conscious mind we would be without electrical light and power, something that we all use and take for granted in our day to day lives.

Do you think I could have authored this book without using my conscious and subconscious mind? I used my mind and heart to write what I thought. The most important thing ever is to BELIEVE IN YOURSELF.

What did you take away from this chapter?

1.

2.

3.

QUARANTINE

Tip #4:

Use your conscious mind to accomplish your goals and enjoy the rewards later.

ALEXA BOWERS

Chapter 5

How We Are More Powerful Together

If we all work together and make peace between each other, then maybe, just maybe, we could all solve more problems in the world. If we all come together then we can truly create some amazing things. I know that Covid – 19 has changed a lot, but that does not mean that we must stop living our lives. If you think just one person can help, imagine more people all working together to make a change. We can make an enormous difference if we just listen to each other's ideas and thoughts. There is only one Earth, and we need to take care of it together.

If we all put our ideas together then we could solve so many more things, like pollution, climate change and more. If

QUARANTINE

you just listen to others and believe in yourself, then we can do great things. All we need to do is work together, work hard, and believe in ourselves. Challenging work will always pay off in the end. During quarantine things were hard, but we all needed to remember to work together. Even though we could not see each other in person, we could still work together by masterminding things on calls, texts, Zoom, FaceTime and more.

    One way people would help each other was by donating to charities or raising money to help others to get through Quarantine. By raising money, it helped people who lost jobs or homes or had limit access to basic supplies. A big part that helped a lot was showing your emotions about how you are feeling and being truthful to one another. Even though we still had to make a lot of things virtual, there were just some people that got everyone's spirits up every day and made people feel better about the situation. These past few years has been harder than most people can remember, and a lot of us have struggled and lost many special people and things. Since we have been working together, we're starting to overcome it.

    If there was no one that had positive thoughts in this world then I don't know how we could have gotten through these tough times. There were always those friends, family and others who have helped so much, but you don't always realize it. Some people who have helped me get through the pandemic were my family and friends. Two people that especially helped me were my mom and my dad because they provided me with food, shelter, love and support.

QUARANTINE

What did you take away from this chapter?

1.

2.

3.

TIP #5

Work together to accomplish big goals quicker and create relationships with one another.

Chapter 6

When You Lose Things You Take for Granted

  Sometimes us humans take people for granted, money for granted, and so much more. We do not always realize how lucky we are until we lose that luck. If you keep using excuses, like "I'll do it tomorrow", you may run out of time and there may not be a "tomorrow". Sometimes we use excuses to get out of the way of doing the hard things, but like my dad always says, if you do the hard things up front life will be easier, but if you do the easy things up front then life may be harder.

Another tip my dad always reminds me is that not every day do we want to eat healthy, not every day do we want to work out, but if we keep saying we will do it the next day, there eventually will not be a next day. I know that there are sometimes that people just do not want to do the right thing. Some days you may feel tired or have something else you want to do rather than going to see a family member. However, that loved one may not always be there and one thing you can't get back is time, so make sure to cherish the moment and use your time wisely.

I realized during the pandemic all the things I was grateful for because sometimes I was close to losing a loved one. It was not always because of COVID-19, but when this all happened, I started really thinking about how some people do not have the things I have, and that started to make me feel thankful. The best way to avoid taking things for granted is to just take a couple minutes out of your day and think of all the things that you are thankful for. Even if you have an extra minute just call some of those loved ones or friends and thank them.

There are some people who would not wear masks or care about getting with Covid. Some people just did not care about what others said when they told them to please put on your mask. What those people didn't realize is that if they are not being careful, it could result in a loved one getting very

QUARANTINE

sick, then they could pass away just because you did not want to wear a mask or sanitize.

    This year made me realize that I took school for granted because in the past there were days I didn't wanted to go into school or days I just didn't feel like waking up to go virtually or go in person. But then I realized there are people in 2020 that never got the chance to step inside their school, or see their friends, or meet their teachers in person, or like me, who started 2020 in a new school.

    I didn't always think that having the ability to go back to school was such a big privilege, but then I saw how many students stayed virtual the entire year and never got to experience school that year in person. Then I started saying that I'm going to wake up and put in the effort to be able to go to school in person again.

What did you take away from this chapter?

1.
_____
_____
_____
_____

2.
_____
_____
_____
_____

3.
_____
_____
_____
_____

TIP #6:

Remind yourself of all of the things you have to be grateful for. Even things that you may think are simple, like food and water, don't come as easily to others, so be grateful for all the little things!

Chapter 7

How Reading & Writing Helps You Feed Your Brain

Reading has not only helped me throughout quarantine, but I know it's also helped others. I know I do not always want to do it and I'm sure not everyone always wants to take the time out of their day when they could be watching TV or playing with friends, instead of reading a book. When you take that time out of your day, just a couple minutes to think and learn something new, you will feel more accomplished.

During quarantine, reading and writing my thoughts down on paper helped me be able to have a better mindset

QUARANTINE

and to even help me write this book because if it wasn't for reading and doing my research on how other authors wrote and told stories then I could not have written this book. If it wasn't for reading, some things will be much harder like even if you're just reading a magazine, news article, and keeping up with all this covid stuff you are still learning.

Not only is reading good for your mind and body but it can also help you expand your mind and learn new things. Reading can sometimes touch your heart, break your heart and just make you think and really connect with what you're reading. No matter what you're reading you can always learn something new. Not only from business or current event books and articles, but anything you're reading there is always a purpose and something behind it. Also, there are some books we do not always want to read, but sometimes you just have to think about why the person would have written what they wrote unless it had to do with something they experienced, heard about or saw. Reading has helped my dad to become an amazing dad and business owner.

I don't know how much you're reading or the exact amount of people that make reading part of their daily routine, but I do know that reading will always help feed your brain and this knowledge will help you daily in life. I know that there are more fun things to do than reading, but like I have mentioned before, if you do the hard things first then life will be easier, but if you do the easy things first then life may be harder.

Believe me, as a kid I would not always choose reading, but if you start to read and journal your thoughts when you're young, your brain will be stronger, give yourself a sense of accomplishment and you'll be more knowledgeable by the time you're an adult. My dad always tells me every day that he wishes that he would have read more when he was younger. Since he didn't read a lot, he now has to start later in life, which is harder, but not impossible. It's never too late to make a positive change in your daily habits.

Even for adults I know it's hard to take time out of your day to go pick up a book, but what's stopping you from picking up that book? Think about that. There are lots of excuses that we can make up, but we have to admit if they're good or bad. Kids' excuses are usually that "I don't want to," or that "I don't need to." For adults the excuse can be, "I'm tired," or "I don't have enough time," or "I work, so I don't need to read." These are all excuses that are stopping us from achieving our goals. I know I use excuses too, and no one's perfect, but why do you have enough time to watch a show or sit down and be lazy, but you don't have enough time to pick up a book and journal your thoughts?

QUARANTINE

What did you take away from this chapter?

1.

2.

3.

TIP #7:

Reading and writing helps you so much more than you may think it does in life, in everything from sending a text to speaking at a job interview. Always value reading!

Chapter 8

How Balance Was Important

It was important to have balance while quarantined. Not only with health, reading or staying active, but in general there were many ways it was important. For example, you have to balance how much food you are eating to stay in shape and stay healthy. You also had to stay balanced with your schedule by making sure that, while at home, you were still getting work done. You had to make sure you weren't just sitting around and being lazy, but you were trying to pick up a book or learn something new

There were many ways that balance was important. Some people may have had trouble being balanced in all of the categories mentioned. For instance, I wasn't always balanced, but then I started to become more balanced as time went on.

The first couple weeks I was not very balanced with my health, and I wasn't in shape or eating the right foods. Then I remembered that I should start training my body and my mind to get ready for upcoming sports. Even though we were in quarantine, and we had to stay at our house, I had to find ways to stay at home but still train my mind and my body to be ready for the new year. Once we started getting farther into quarantine, I would make time to outside by going for runs, walks and bike rides with my family. I also started to have balanced meals again, by pre-planning what to eat.

One way I stayed balanced in my mind was that I meditated, did yoga, and I read books and quotes with my dad. Sometimes my dad and I would also journal while reading and write down three things we learned about that chapter. Doing this helped me to train my mind. Once I got back to school, I started thinking better and asking myself more questions and it helped me a lot.

Balance is a very important thing, but it was even more important during quarantine because you could get off-balance or use things like excuses to get out of doing what you really needed to do. I know that not everyone wanted to train their mind and workout, but you have to remember, there were some people who took the time to work on themselves during quarantine and some who decided to do nothing.

QUARANTINE

We had to manage actions, habits and excuses to stay balance. In life, we all have the same choices but only we can decide what we do with our time. We figured out that during Covid we had more time than ever, and balance became even more of challenge because we had more time on our hands.

There were some days I was did not pick the right things to do and other days we picked rights things to do to achieve our goals or have fun. It's easy to get off tract and not working closer to something in life you want. We learned to enjoy the journey and keep working on getting better each day. We learned balance is tricky thing and you have to focus on balance in your personal life by having fun and balance in achieving your goals. There were some days I was one of those people that would just sit around, but there were other days when I'd get up and get ready to face the world.

What did you take away from this chapter?

1.

2.

3.

QUARANTINE

TIP #8:

Balance keeps you mentally, physically, and socially healthy. Try to balance out the activities through your day. For example, if you spend three hours riding your bike, spend the next three resting and catching up with friends.

Chapter 9

Using the Pandemic as an Excuse

A global pandemic can be a really good excuse to get out of doing things. For example, people would use the pandemic as an excuse for bad grades in school, or not being able to accomplish their goals. Also, there are some people that say that the pandemic has been holding them back, but they've just been holding themselves back by using the pandemic as an excuse. There is not only one age group that has used the pandemic as an excuse, but everyone has.

Now it's different if you're sick with something and you physically can't do it, but if you're just choosing not to do it or not having a good mindset when you are well enough, it's just an excuse. Excuses are a very hard thing to recognize when

QUARANTINE

you're using them. You could just be like, "I'm tired," but, you're just making yourself and your mind even more tired by not getting up and doing something.

There is a difference between an excuse and a reason. A reason would be that you broke your ankle so you can't go on a run. An excuse would be that you just don't want to, or you're too tired to go on a run. I always try to ask myself, am I using an excuse, or do I have a reason why I'm not doing this? You may think that a reason would be that you can't go on a run because you have a dentist appointment. Well, you're right you can't go now, but you can always go later. What's stopping you from doing it later?

Make sure in life that you find the person or people who can help you through the tough choices and decisions, and are always there for you and help you make good choices. These types of people were especially important during quarantine because they're the people who will keep you going and guided you away from making excuses. Sometimes those types of people are hard to find but just because they're hard to find doesn't mean that they're impossible to find. For example, the people that I found pushing me to try my best and do my best were my parents, friends, and family.

I know that my true friends will always be there for me and push me to my limits. I'm not saying that you need to find those people right away, but you will find them someday.

ALEXA BOWERS

Especially during the pandemic to be a good person, it was important to be the encouraging person that could hold you accountable and trust you. For example, those people to me were my parents and I was that for them.

I would like you to think of one excuse that you have used over the pandemic, or just one excuse that you've ever used. Then, I'd like you to think of one good reason that you've used. Now if you really think about differences in your excuse and reason, then you'll be able to find out what are excuses and what are reasons. Believe me, no one is perfect, and if you're trying so hard to never use an excuse again. It probably won't happen because you're always going to use excuses. You just need to recognize if it's a bad excuse, or a good reason.

The most important thing that you can do is practice noticing when you have these bad excuses. An example of a bad excuse is if, let's say, you have a friend and it's their birthday, and of course you're invited to the birthday party. But your enemy is also invited to the party, and that enemy is friends with your friend. Then you use an excuse saying that you can't make it because you're not feeling well, but you're just not going just because your enemy is going to be there. Now that's a bad excuse, and you're being selfish by not going to see your friend on his or her birthday. We don't always don't realize that excuses sometimes don't just affect ourselves but can also affect others.

QUARANTINE

What did you take away from this chapter?

1.

2.

3.

TIP #9:

Excuses are just a way of putting off the things you want to accomplish. Start saying YES and do it!

Chapter 10

Quarantine Coming to an End

In conclusion, Quarantine 2020 to 2021 was a weird time, but not only bad things have come out of it; lots of lessons have come out of it. Quarantine has taught me not to take things for granted, and to cherish the moments that you have with others. I have also learned the difference between excuses and reasons. Another thing that I'm very happy I learned was how to balance between different things, like family, friends, school, and sports.

    I hope that during the pandemic that you took that time to either learn something or achieve something that you always wanted to do. So, you now know that this book is not only about quarantine but is also about focusing on yourself more or focusing on others more. Another reason why I wanted to write about the pandemic is because of how much I've learned or realized during all of this.

If you're thinking to yourself, "Wow, I never knew any of this, or learned any of this," what's stopping you from doing or achieving your goal now? Make sure to always remember that we are more powerful together than apart. You may not think that we're more powerful together, but there are many ways that we have all been powerful together. One way is that we all joined together and socially distanced, sacrificed many valuable things, lost things, and wore masks. Now, did all of us have to do this? The answer is "No," but we did it anyway, and because of that we made a difference.

If you read this book until the end, that means you were trying to find something. Some of you may be thinking, "so what?" or "this doesn't affect me," but many things that we don't think impact others actually do. Like, even just a couple people going into a store or being unsafe and getting the disease can spread to many other people and cause deaths and tragedies. You may think that just because something hasn't happened to you, that nothing ever will, but it's important to listen to your heart and end up making a good choice.

I know sometimes it's hard to make the right choice and, even if you may not realize it at the time, there's always going to be a better way to do something. Taking time to think

QUARANTINE

and reflect you will know what that way is. Some people may also think that you don't need to know about things that have happened in the past, but when you're aware of the history, then we can always make something better because you can learn from the mistakes that have already happened.

"You must learn from the mistakes of others. You can't possibly live long enough to make them all yourself"

Samuel Levenson

You did not have to read this book, but you made a choice and hopefully you see there's always a reason behind your choices. You just need to find that reason and some people may have stopped reading at this point, but you made a good choice to keep reading. You know why you made a good choice? Because you probably found out many things that you didn't know were important before.

Something else that will always be important and was not only important during quarantine was having a good mindset, and to believe that a good mindset leads to a good life and good health. Because health is not only the physical part, but it is also about mental and social parts. If you don't have those three things down, then you're not ultimately healthy.

ALEXA BOWERS

To wrap it up, quarantine would not be everyone's idea of a perfect year, I think it was far from what most would consider perfect, but it was still an amazing year for me. I learned so many things, like how to write a book, for starters. I also learned the importance of family and surrounding yourself with good people. So, thank you pandemic, for a year we will all never forget, but also a year I learned a lot about myself and that we are all capable of achieving anything we set our mind to.

QUARANTINE

What did you take away from this chapter?

1.
_____
_____
_____
_____

2.
_____
_____
_____
_____

3.
_____
_____
_____
_____

FINAL TIP:

Always be sure to make thought-out choices, and create your own path, while being your own confident self.

ABOUT THE AUTHOR

Alexa Bowers was just 11 years old when she started writing the book *Quarantined*. She finished the book at age 12, and has always written well in school, even earning a Distinguished Honor Roll (the award for getting straight A's the school year 2020-2021). In the future she hopes to get into the real estate business with her parents.

She developed a love for tennis by playing with her dad, and has a passion for basketball, baking, cooking, and spending time with her friends, family, and dog Bella. She loves creating stories and new ideas, and reading stories with her mom growing up, which was a huge inspiration for this book.